# The Philosophy of the LostxRabbitt and Brimstone and Bandit part 1

David Ballinger

Published by David Ballinger, 2024.

While every precaution has been taken in the preparation of this book, the publisher assumes no responsibility for errors or omissions, or for damages resulting from the use of the information contained herein.

THE PHILOSOPHY OF THE LOSTXRABBITT AND BRIMSTONE AND BANDIT PART 1

Dedicated to all my former partners (Past and future).

# Introduction

*You can't teach someone something they think they already know. The way this work is received by the reader will justify or invalidate the previous statement.*

*People often take issue with the idea of learning from someone else. Sadly, more and more people perceive the position of a student as a demotion in status or the inferior party in the process of learning or as demeaning. In the worst cases, insulting. This misconception is tragic and damaging to the individual and society in general.*

*A prime example of this is when the apprentice or novice is being trained; they will often respond with "I know" when they believe the instructor is seeing them as ignorant or naïve.*

*The elevated position that the student had enjoyed throughout the ages has been diminished by the systemic rise of egocentric masters who desire acknowledgment for their own achievements and the effort they themselves have put into acquiring said knowledge. This is precisely what prevents the instructor from achieving true mastery of the skill they have supposedly mastered, internally degrading the very art that they claim to love.*

*The true master knows that by elevating the student, they will succeed in passing on their beloved craft, ultimately creating an opportunity to improve said craft through the student. Not with the fear that their student will surpass their own skill but instead with the hope the pupil will do exactly that. In the mind of a true master, this is the very purpose of passing on their legacy in the first place. Legacy is the master's reward for their efforts, not the instant gratification of praise or the perceived admiration of the masses.*

*PHILOSOPHY OF THE LOST RABBIT: YOU ARE YOUR FAULT*

*Everyone gets exactly what they want all the time, every time. Otherwise, you would do something different to change what you get. No one has anything happen to them by surprise. You knew it was a possibility, whatever it was when you consciously set the events in motion beforehand. You can claim you don't know why it happened, and those like you may pretend to believe you. But we all know why everything happens to us when it happens. We all know why we get what we get, good or bad. Whether it was welcome or unwelcome. We asked for it and we got it.*

*Review*

*The opening sets a tone of personal responsibility, urging readers to reflect on the intentional nature of their experiences.*

## *YOU ARE YOUR FAULT*

*You are where you are because of the choices you made. You are who you are because of the choices you made. Your life is what it is because of the choices you made. If you don't like where you are, change the choices you make. If you don't like who you are, change the choices you make. If you don't like your life, change the choices you make. You can't change the past, but you can change the choices you make in the present, which will change your future. You are not a victim of circumstance; you are a product of your choices. You are not a prisoner of fate; you are a prisoner of your decisions. You are not a helpless pawn in the game of life; you are the player making the moves. Take responsibility for your*

*choices. Stop blaming others for where you are, who you are, and how your life is. You are your fault.*

*Review*

*This statement reinforces the overarching theme of personal responsibility, urging readers to acknowledge the impact of their choices on their present circumstances. It rejects the victim mentality, emphasizing the power individuals have to shape their destinies through mindful decision-making. The concise yet powerful message encapsulates the core philosophy of personal accountability presented throughout the musings.*

*FIX YOURSELF FOR YOURSELF*

*If you want something genuine in your life then stop being fake. If you want truth in your relationship and in life then stop lying. If you want to be loved for who you are then stop picking a mate because you think they're hot. If you don't like the rumors going around about you then spread better ones. If you keep telling everyone you're a good person, then you're not. It's ok because your friends probably aren't either.*

*Review*

*This part delivers straightforward advice on authenticity and self-improvement. It advocates for aligning actions with true desires, reinforcing the theme of personal responsibility.*

*SELF-ESTEEM FRAUD*

*So tired of hearing people tell others they have to love themselves more and constantly vomiting up this crap self-help philosophy of self-love. They claim that loving yourself more is the cure for all mental and emotional illness. SELF-LOVE IS THE PROBLEM. Drug addiction and most emotional problems are the result of too much self-love, not the lack of it. The feeling that you can do whatever drug you want as much as you want without consequence is born of self-love. The feeling you're alone or in an unsatisfying relationship is also the product of too much self-love. The selfish and entitled attitude that all good feelings and relationships should be yours no matter your actions is, by definition, self-love. Only through denying self and learning how to tell yourself no will you be able to love or be worthy of receiving real love. Serve others and their needs, and get yourself out of your way so God can take care of you and your needs.*

*Review*

*This part challenges the prevailing self-help narrative around self-love, asserting that excessive self-love contributes to various issues. It proposes a counterintuitive approach, advocating for self-denial and prioritizing others for genuine love.*

*EMOTIONAL VACCINATION :*

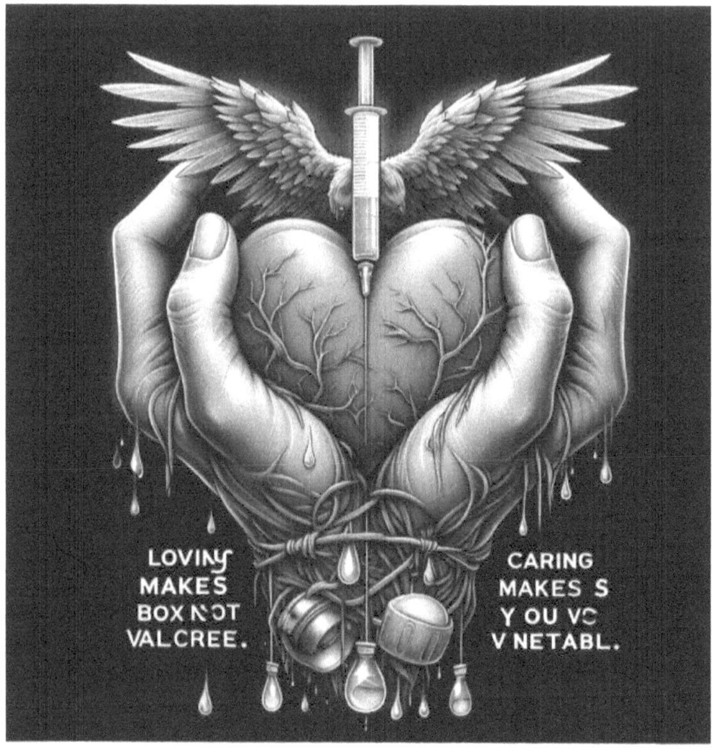


*LOVE BUT DO NOT CARE. LOVING MAKES YOU STRONG. CARING MAKES YOU VULNERABLE.*

*Review*

*This segment introduces a paradoxical concept, distinguishing between love and care. It suggests that love strengthens while excessive care renders one vulnerable, offering a pragmatic approach to emotional dynamics.*

## *GOD HAS A PLAN*

*God does have a plan for your life. In fact, He has a plan for everyone's life. The problem is: most of you don't like His plan for your life. You think His plan is for you to be rich and famous. Or powerful and influential. Or happy and content. You think God's plan is for you to have everything you want and for everything to go your way. News flash: It's not. God's plan is for you to learn how to love. Love is self-sacrifice. Love is doing what's best for others no matter what it costs you. Love is giving up what you want so others can have what they need. Love is giving up your life for others. Not just dying for them, but living for them. It's sacrificing your dreams, your desires, your wants, your needs, your plans, your agenda, and your preferences for others. God's plan is for you to learn how to love like He loves. If you're not doing that, you're not following His plan. You're following your own plan. Which is why your life sucks and everything goes wrong. If you're not willing to sacrifice what you want for others, why should God sacrifice what He wants for you? God's plan is to love others through you. If you're not doing that, you're not following His plan for your life.*

*Review*

*This segment delves into the concept of God's plan, challenging common misconceptions about it. It emphasizes the central theme of love as self-sacrifice, presenting a profound perspective on the purpose of life and divine intentions. The review recognizes the philosophical depth and thought-provoking nature of the content.*

## *PRAGMATIC PEP TALK?*

*Your true love is not waiting somewhere out there. The friend you want doesn't want to know you. Your dog is going to die way before you do... There is no silver lining or light at the end of a tunnel... There is only you and that's okay because that's all you really care about anyway... If you think God put you here to be happy, you have a lot of growing up to do. Show me one happy ending or happy beginning for that matter anywhere in the bible. You can't! He even came down himself and lived a miserable life and died horribly just to show you it can be done without lying, cheating, stealing, oh yeah or whining. Jeez, get a clue. Life doesn't get better or easier with time only your ability to withstand the pain of life improves. You don't get hardened steel with happy thoughts and candy cane dreams. It takes a hammer and extreme heat to make a sharp sword as it takes pain and misery to achieve a sharp mind and the wisdom to realize everything is as it should be...*

*Review*

*This segment presents a pragmatic perspective, challenging conventional notions of true love and happiness. It draws from biblical references to underscore the harsh realities of life, advocating for resilience in the face of challenges.*

# Get Over It'

## GET OVER IT

*Life doesn't get better or easier as you trudge through it. Not for you, not for anyone... The only thing that improves is your ability to deal with it... Life doesn't get better or easier as you trudge through it. Not for you, not for anyone... The only thing that improves is your ability to deal with it...*

*Review*

*This repetitive yet impactful section hammers home the central message that life doesn't inherently get better. It emphasizes the continuous improvement of one's ability to cope with life's challenges.*

*SLOWDOWN HOTROD*

*The problem with relationships today is, shit gets physical too fast and shit gets exclusive too fast before you realize you don't even like this person. Before you get a chance to know who they are, you're stuck in a commitment before you realize they're a deviant or an unfaithful personality type. Who may be lying to themselves but are surely lying to you. Knowing these facts won't stop you from doing it again.*

*Review*

*This segment addresses the pace of modern relationships, cautioning against committing before truly understanding a*

*person. It highlights the potential mismatch between physical
intimacy and genuine connection.*

"You think?  - overthinking in relationships"
the  philissophy of the lost rabbtiebpit,

*YOU THINK?*

*If you think you've found it. Think again. If you think it's the real
thing. Think again. If you think it's gonna be different this time,
think again. If you think it's gonna last forever, think about not
thinking anymore and just get a dog. Because thinking obviously
isn't your thing.*

*Review*

*This part injects humor into the discussion, using sarcasm to caution against idealistic assumptions about love. The suggestion to get a dog serves as a lighthearted alternative, questioning the feasibility of finding lasting love.*

*BRIGHT SIDE*

*If you didn't have what you thought you had then you lose nothing when it's gone.*

*Review*

*This segment introduces a positive outlook, emphasizing the potential lack of loss when something falsely perceived is gone. It encourages embracing the absence of what was believed to be real, offering a perspective shift from loss to liberation*

.

BRIGHT SIDE
THE LOSING SOMETHIINGG NEVER
LNEREH/AD
IN IESULTIMS
IS REISHI
IIS NO REAL LOSS.
LIFE
LIGHT
PHILOSOPHY OF LOST RABBIT

*NOT AGAIN*

*Never think your above being fooled by the dark lord; he always has a more advanced agent waiting for you to drop your guard, for you to be receptive to yet another load of bullshit. Once again convincing you it's different this time and your true love has finally arrived. The great sex Is almost enough to convince you once again, but just in case it's not; the next one is always smarter and a better, more poisonous version than the last and ultimately more destructive to your life and mind than any and every conniving bitch or evil asshole you've ever been fool enough to become involved with. Yet time and time again you walk face-first into another soul-crushing, life-draining relationship like a cartoon coyote thinking he's finally gonna catch that fucking roadrunner and enjoy a well-deserved dinner. Only to*

*have the ground disappear beneath you and the 100-ton boulder that is reality land on your head after you hit the ground.*

*Review*

*This section delves into the perpetual cycle of falling into damaging relationships despite past experiences. The analogy of the cartoon coyote chasing the roadrunner adds a humorous yet poignant touch to the exploration of repeated mistakes.*

## SARCASTIC FOOL

*There is no reason for me to doubt you and no one is out to betray me. Though. You do realize that actions and devotion are how trust is earned. Like risking your ass for another or rejecting rejection despite someone telling you they don't love you anymore. It is not like I have ever had any reason to doubt you in the past, so... like you said... my paranoia is unfounded. Because you have always had my back no matter what, and you apologized for when you didn't, then swore you wouldn't do it again, again. Except you did it again five minutes ago. But that doesn't mean anything. It's not like it's a pattern I should be aware and beware of. ◈ So I'll just drink the Kool-Aid and use the light to move forward into the catastrophes that are undoubtedly coming. As long as you have the gas to keep the light on, I'll be behind you until it gets dangerous; then I'll take my place in the front, not to lead but to bear the brunt of the coming onslaught. To protect the torchbearer. So that when the mistakes have painful consequences and are then proven to be the product of you not listening to me, that information can be properly ignored to prevent it from not happening again.*

*Review*

*This segment adopts a sarcastic tone, delving into trust issues and the cyclical nature of broken promises. The humor adds depth to the critique of blind trust.*

*BUT YOU...?*

*Someone tells you "I heard this and I heard that about you and so and so says you did this or you did that." You say, "Let me explain what really happened." They cut you off and say, "I don't want to get involved."*

*Review*

*This part confronts the frustration of being misunderstood and unheard, highlighting the challenges of trying to clarify rumors or misinformation. It exposes the futility of explaining oneself in certain situations.*

*FUTILE*

*If you have to explain to someone why something they did is obviously messed up, you've wasted your time. If they say they understand and apologize, well... they're lying. If you believe them and accept their apology, well then you're a fool. If you repeat this cycle more than once, you're in love with a psycho and you're wasting your life.*

*Review*

*This segment emphasizes the fruitlessness of explaining the obvious, pointing out the potential insincerity in apologies. It escalates to a stark warning about repetitive cycles, urging self-awareness in relationships.*

*JUST SAYIN*

*If Love Will find a Way and love conquers all and love is the answer. Then why does hate always seem so much more satisfying*

*Review*

*This segment questions the conventional wisdom about love, juxtaposing it with the seemingly more satisfying nature of hate. It adds a layer of skepticism to common romantic ideals, introducing a thought-provoking perspective on the complexities of human emotions.*

*REAL WHAT?*

*I READ A POST THAT SAID REAL RELATIONSHIPS REAL LOVE AND REAL CARING IS RARE... To that, I responded: All of those things are illusions. Unless you remove yourself from the equation. Too often all of the real things you just described are just labels your very real pride puts on abstract concepts to make them seem real and strictly personal. For example: real love for me, real loyalty to me, and real respect for me or a real relationship with me. They are only real to you if they anoint you as the primary beneficiary or majority stockholder. Those same ideas that have remained fundamentally honored by the other party are quickly rejected as fake or disingenuous as soon as YOUR concept of REAL has been violated. "on't waste your time seeking something that is so rare and so sought after that to find it would be akin to discovering*

*the Holy Grail or the Ark of the Covenant. To put it bluntly:
You are the only one who can give these "real" things to anyone
because you are the only one who "really" even knows what they
are... to you.*

*Review*

*This section challenges the rarity of genuine relationships,
emphasizing subjective perspectives and the self-centric nature of
defining 'real' love and caring. It urges readers not to seek the
elusive and rare, presenting a pragmatic outlook.*

*FLY ON THE WALL*

*Just once I'd like to see the look on someone's face when they
realize they should have listened to me. Then watch it again
when they realize it's too late; I'm already gone.*

*Review*

*This section captures the desire to witness the realization of the
importance of advice, adding a touch of drama to the narrative.
The metaphor of being a fly on the wall emphasizes the yearning
for others to comprehend the wisdom shared.*

*PITY THE FOOL*

*You think it sucks to be betrayed or wronged by a lowlife piece of shit... Imagine being that lowlife piece of shit... Then be grateful you're not one. UNLESS you are one. Then go fuck yourself.*

*Review*

*This part delivers a blunt reality check, prompting gratitude for not being the perpetrator in betrayals or wrongdoings. It concludes with a straightforward message for those who may indeed be the lowlife piece of the puzzle.*

*Conclusion*

*Instead of asking "What is the meaning of life?" Consider: That life is the meaning of what.*

# T*HE* *END*

## *TEASER*

### *Brimstone and Bandit*

Brimstone and Bandit:

# Chapter 1: The Embers of Wrath

In the desolate landscape of Dragon's Hollow, where shadows danced with flames to some apocalyptic tune. A lone dragon, orphaned and enraged, soared through the night sky. Born of the fire and rage that only cruelty breeds, the creature, known as Brimstone, clung to his burning desire for retribution against the architect of his misery —King Slagathon and his unholy Knights of Hellskeep.

# DAVID BALLINGER

With scales dark as the ashes of his ruined past, Brimstone cast a malevolent silhouette against the moonlit horizon. The dragons massive wings, once a symbol of his freedom, now bore the scars of battles fought and losses endured. His heart, a cauldron of anger and sorrow, fueled his relentless pursuit of justice.

As Brimstone unleashed his fiery wrath upon the poverty-stricken villages surrounding King Slagathons' castle, he left a trail of devastation in his wake. Flames danced like vengeful spirits as they consumed the thatched roofed hovels stealing what little remained of the hopes the poor peasants dared cling too.

Amidst the chaos, Brimstone's fiery gaze fell upon a small, surviving soul—a lone puppy, with fur as black as the dragon's heart. The pup trembled beneath the dragon's looming shadow. As Brimstone prepared to deliver a final blow, a flicker of curiosity crossed the dragon's eyes.

IN THAT FLEETING MOMENT, as Brimstone raised his clawed talon, Bandit, the tiny survivor, opened one eye and gazed up at the fearsome dragon. A silent plea echoed in the pup's sad, innocent gaze, and Brimstone found himself unexpectedly captivated by the vulnerability of this small creature.

The dragon's heart, though hardened by years of bitterness, softened in the presence of Bandit's innocence. A sudden realization swept over Brimstone: in sparing the life of this defenseless puppy, he had spared a fragment of his own dwindling empathy.

As the moon hung heavy in the night sky, Brimstone, conflicted and haunted by the memories of his past, made an unexpected choice. With a reluctant snort of smoke, he turned away from the village, leaving behind a legacy of destruction. In the darkness, Brimstone and Bandit embarked on an unforeseen journey, bound by an unlikely companionship that would challenge the very foundations of the dragon's quest for revenge.

# Chapter 2: Unlikely Companions

Brimstone, the wrathful dragon, soared through the moonlit night, the memory of the village's smoldering ruins haunting his thoughts. Unbeknownst to him, the small black-furred puppy, Bandit, trailed behind, determined to keep pace with the massive creature that had spared his life.

Snorts of smoke billowed from Brimstone's nostrils as he attempted to discourage the persistent pup, but Bandit, undeterred, pressed on. Through desolate landscapes and over jagged peaks, the unlikely duo forged a silent bond – a silent pact between a vengeful dragon and a tenacious pup.

UPON REACHING THE CAVERNOUS lair nestled within the heart of Dragon's Hollow, Brimstone, exhausted from his fiery exploits, decided it was time to part ways with his unexpected companion. With a final snort of smoke and a dismissive flick of his tail, he attempted to convey his desire for solitude.

However, Bandit, displaying a tenacity matched only by his cuteness, refused to be cast aside. The pup continued to follow his unlikely savior, navigating the rocky terrain with determined little steps.

Amused and irritated in equal measure, the conflicted reptile couldn't help but marvel at Bandit's resilience. Brimstone, unused to companionship of any kind, found himself engaged in a annoying dance with the persistent pup. Brimstone's snorts of annoyance were met with wagging tails and playful barks from Bandit.

As they finally entered the cavern, the mood shifted from irritation to amusement. Brimstone, accustomed to the solitude of his lair, found himself in a quarrel with Bandit over sleeping arrangements. The dragon's cavernous abode echoed with their banter, each trying to claim their own space.

BRIMSTONE HAD FINALLY succumbed to exhaustion from the day's events. As he settled into a comfortable nook he cast a disapproving glare at the persistent pup.

Yet, as the dragon drifted into a restless slumber, he awoke to an unexpected warmth beneath his wing. Opening one eye, Brimstone discovered Bandit curled up, nestled snugly against his formidable form. Disgust and surprise flickered across his scaly face, but a strange sense of contentment tugged at the corners of his heart.

In that peculiar moment, Brimstone's hardened exterior softened, and a rare smile graced his draconic visage. With a reluctant chuckle, he conceded defeat to the determined pup. As they lay side by side, dragon and pup, beneath the shadowy embrace of Dragon's Hollow, an unspoken bond emerged – a bond forged in the unlikely alliance between a vengeful dragon and the survivor who refused to be left behind.

# Chapter 3

As Brimstone and Bandit traversed the haunting landscapes of Dragon's Hollow, an unexpected flood of memories gripped the vengeful dragon. In the shadows of his tortured past, a vivid recollection unfolded—a tale of betrayal, loss, and an unforeseen twist that would forever intertwine Brimstone's fate with Bandit's. In the tranquility of a moonlit night, Brimstone found himself compelled to share the painful fragments of his origin. As his deep voice resonated through the desolate surroundings, he recounted the harrowing night when King Slagathon and his Knights of Hellskeep descended upon Brimstone's peaceful nest.

THE DRAGON'S EYES GLAZED over as he vividly relived the brutality of that night—the merciless flames, the clash of swords, and the anguished cries of his parents. In the heart-wrenching recollection, Brimstone's mother fought valiantly to protect her precious hatchling from the marauding Invaders. As the chaos unfolded, a twist of fate revealed itself. In a courageous act, two kanine bystanders where unwitting observers of the unfolding battle. They intervened and with the ferocity borne of desperation, the female snatched the defenseless baby Brimstone from the fiery chaos, cradling him in her mouth. Brimstone, still a mere hatchling, clung to life as he witnessed the world unraveling around him. As the dragon recounted this pivotal moment, he described a medallion that swung from the Valiant dogs neck—a keltic cross that dangled with each determined movement. It became clear that this emblem, a symbol of strength and protection, had been a beacon of hope during the darkest hours of Brimstone's infancy.

MIDWAY THROUGH BRIMSTONE'S narrative, Bandit, driven by an inexplicable sense of recognition, shook his neck. Amidst the tangled mane of black fur, a glimmer of metal caught the moonlight—a keltic cross medallion, the same described by Brimstone as hanging from his rescuers neck during the escape from the battle.

In that poignant moment, realization dawned on both Brimstone and Bandit. The medallion, once a symbol of protection and sacrifice, now hung from Bandit's neck, revealing the profound connection between the dragon's harrowing past and the pup's courageous lineage. Brimstone's recounting of that fateful bynight reached its climax as the dragon described how Bandit's parents had intervened, rescuing the vulnerable hatchling from the clutches of King Slagathons' brutality. The medallion, a silent witness to the heroic act, had found its way into Bandit's possession, unknowingly linking the two companions in a tale of intertwined destinies. The revelation hung in the air, heavy with the weight of shared history. Bandit, the survivor who refused to be left behind, carried not only the spirit of his parents but also the tangible emblem of their bravery—a medallion that had once swung from his mother's neck as she cradled baby Brimstone in her mouth, shielding him from the flames of vengeance. As the moon cast its silvery glow over Dragon's Hollow, Brimstone and Bandit stood together, connected by a thread woven from the echoes of tragedy and the resilience of those who dared to defy fate. The keltic cross medallion, now a symbol of enduring companionship and redemption, swung gently from Bandit's neck—a silent testament to the unspoken bond forged in the shadows of Dragon's Hollow.

---- ✥ ----

*THE END*
  *Concept art for Part 2*

---- ✥ ----

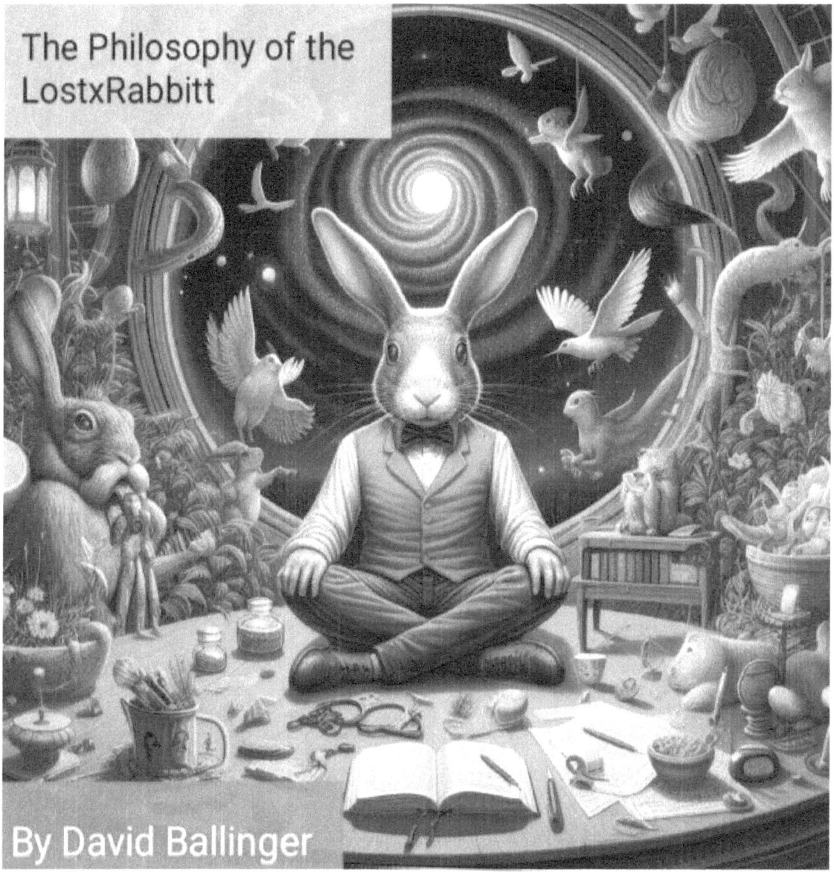

The Philosophy of the
LostxRabbitt
By David Ballinger

The Philosophy of the
LostxRabbitt

The Philosophy of the LostxRabbitt
Eating Crow for the Soul
By Tate Michealson

# Don't miss out!

Visit the website below and you can sign up to receive emails whenever David Ballinger publishes a new book. There's no charge and no obligation.

https://books2read.com/r/B-A-QGDKB-PQJID

Connecting independent readers to independent writers.

Did you love *The Philosophy of the LostxRabbitt and Brimstone and Bandit part 1*? Then you should read *The Philosophy of the LostxRabbitt*[1] by David Ballinger!

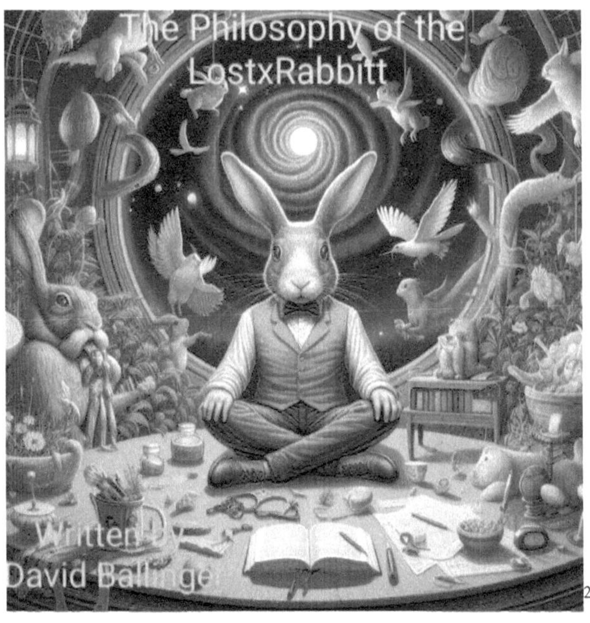


[2]

root of many problems rather than the solution. It advocates self-denial and prioritization of others instead.

Religious themes emerge as well, offering an unorthodox perspective on God's plan centering around self-sacrifice and service to others rather than personal fulfillment. It uses biblical references to emphasize the inherent struggles of life.

Overall, the piece does not aim to inspire or offer solace. Instead, it adopts a defiant, provocative posture designed to shatter comforting illusions and conventional thinking about love, life purpose, and

---

1. https://books2read.com/u/mVnyyp

2. https://books2read.com/u/mVnyyp

personal growth. Its blunt intellectual honesty is both refreshing and unsettling, forcing deep self-reflection.